Just Us Girls™ guide to Effortless Entertaining

To

From

Just Us Girls guide to Effortless Entertaining

Copyright © 1999 FrontPorch Books,
a division of Garborg's LLC
Published by Garborg's LLC
P. O. Box 20132, Bloomington, MN 55420

Written by Julie Sutton and Angela Jarecki
Illustrated by Angela Jarecki

Design by Lecy Design

Scripture quotations marked NIV are taken from the Holy Bible, New International Version®.
Copyright © 1973, 1978, 1984 by International Bible Society.
Used by permission of Zondervan Publishing House.

Scripture quotations marked TLB are taken from The Living Bible © 1971.
Used by permission of Tyndale House Publishers, Inc., Wheaton, Illinois 60189.
All rights reserved.

All rights reserved. No part of this publication may be reproduced,
stored in a retrieval system or transmitted in any form by any
means—electronic, mechanical, photocopying, recording, or any
other—except for brief quotations in printed reviews, without
the prior written permission of the publisher.

ISBN 1-58375-472-5
Printed in Mexico

Just Us Girls™ guide to Effortless Entertaining

Written by Julie Sutton
and Angela Jarecki
Illustrated by Angela Jarecki

FrontPorch
BOOKS

VASE

Do you pronounce this word to rhyme with a) "face" or b) "Oz"?

If you said "a," chances are this book is for you! If you answered "b" we're probably not in your league. If you remarked, "My, what a lovely 16th century Venetian urn!" we're not even on the same planet.

Contents

Introduction p.9

Chapter 1
Hospitality "Just Us Girls" Style: The Art of Hanging Out p.11

Chapter 2
Ready, Set...Hyperventilate: Preparing to Entertain p.19

Chapter 3
Girls Just Wanna Have Fun: All Kinds of Parties p.45

Chapter 4
Eat, Drink and Be Merry—For Tomorrow Somebody's Gotta Clean up this Mess.................................... p.67

Chapter 5
Now We're Cookin'... .... p.77

Chapter 6
If I Take My Elbows Off the Table My Head Will Fall Down: Practical Etiquette for the New Millennium p.93

Chapter 7
As Long as You're Under My Roof... Helping House Guests Feel at Home p.113

Introduction

Have you been searching for the definitive book on entertaining? The one that makes you the envy of hostesses everywhere? That transforms you into someone who makes Martha Stewart appear a bumbling fool by comparison? Well, stop it. Who needs the stress?

This book, on the other hand, is designed to meet you right where you are—especially if where you are is generally as far from the stove and the dustpan as possible. It's not that we don't believe in preparing splendid meals, having a sparkly-clean house and generally making things wonderful for company. Gee, we think maids are great! But if you have to do it yourself, we believe in doing it with minimal effort.

Just Us Girls™ guide to Effortless Entertaining mainly focuses on informal entertaining—because that's the only kind we actually do. No five-star chefs or experts on etiquette were hired as consultants. It's strictly a middle-of-the-road handbook for women like us who desire to do **our** best, but don't feel the need to be **the** best. And though we appreciate the praise of friends and family when we outdo ourselves, if the truth be known we appreciate a good shortcut even more. Hopefully, this book will bring you a little of both.

Chapter 1

Hospitality "Just Us Girls" Style: The Art of Hanging Out

That's Entertainment

First, about the word "entertaining." It's an intimidating word. It sounds like we're expected to put on a top hat and do some fancy dance steps with a cane. That's an immediate turn-off to lots of us. If we think we have to provide eye-popping excitement that will keep them talking for weeks to come, we'll probably opt for a quiet evening alone with a good book.

Entertaining doesn't have to be a song and dance. It's really just getting together with friends. It's a chance to spend time with people we care about and let them get to know the real "us." We hate to see anyone turn away the chance to be with friends because they're worried they can't pull it off "just so."

Invite people because you want to spend some time with them. The meal you serve may be a little less than outstanding, "gracious living" in the guise of fine linen and candles may be missing, the conversation may not once rise above the level of the commonplace, but if you're having a good time, I think your guests will too. A happy host makes a happy guest.

—Ruth Stout

I think I formed my ideas about playing hostess from dressing up in wobbly heels and giving tea parties. Now that I'm all grown up, I don't have an apron to my name! But who needs scones and frilly napkins? We can have just as much fun popping open a can of soda and munching on chips. Bring on the girlfriends!

Holding onto a made-from-scratch ideal in a microwave age? Take it down a notch!

hospitable: from the root words "hospital" and "able"—able to have friends over without needing to be hospitalized afterwards.

True hospitality is not to impress people but to impress upon people that you love them.

We do not remember days, we remember moments.

CESARE PAVESE

If you can treat new guests like old friends, you've discovered the secret to effortless entertaining.

Living for the 'Moment'

In the middle of a noisy evening with some of her best girlfriends, Ann sighs a sentimental sigh and declares, "I'm having a Moment." At first we wonder if there's something we can do for her—does someone need to call 911? But Ann explains that a Moment is one of those special instances, suspended in time, when you look around yourself and realize you are surrounded by people who really mean a lot to you, and you kind of "well up" inside thinking about how much richer your life is for having them. Funny thing about Moments. They never seem to happen when you're stressing over dust bunnies in the corner or striving to reach absolute perfection with dessert. They just seem to show up when you're all wrapped up in the joy of… the Moment.

Hospitality is a form of worship.
—Jewish Proverb

Practice tenderhearted mercy and kindness to others. Don't worry about making a good impression on them.
COLOSSIANS 3:12 TLB

Cherish all your happy moments: they make a fine cushion for old age.

Pleasantest of all ties is the tie of host and guest.

—Aeschylus

Letting go and stepping out of our hospitality comfort zone can mean stepping into a wonderful time. Just think of it as "going the extra smile!"

The thought of playing hostess can terrify the best of us. Do those women who thrive on having a house full of people get the same satisfaction out of having their gums scraped? Or could it be that the point isn't to have a "perfect" party in a "perfect" home, but to just open up our hearts?

Pick what gives you pleasure—and then give it away.

To do great and important tasks, two things are necessary: a plan and not quite enough time.

Chapter 2

Ready, Set...Hyperventilate: Preparing to Entertain

> panic: (pá-nik) A feeling that seizes you between the time you plan an event and when it takes place. A combination of the words "plan" and "manic."

Good Clean Fun

Okay, so what constitutes a messy house? If we stop to think about it, many of us approach cleaning "layer by layer," depending on who's coming and how much time we have. For coffee with the next-door neighbor we take the laundry off the kitchen table. If dear old Aunt "White Glove" Louise calls, we may go as far as dusting the top of the refrigerator—or better yet, offer to meet her at a restaurant!

Let him have all your worries and cares, for he is always thinking about you and watching everything that concerns you.
—1 PETER 5:7 TLB

"Hi, I'm Hope, and I'm a cleanaholic."

A Six-Step Recovery Program for Cleanaholics

(No, we don't have twelve, but with this you'll be halfway there!)

1. Admit that you are powerless over dust bunnies. (Naturally, they are going to multiply. They're bunnies!)

2. Acknowledge that a power greater than yourself can restore you to sanity (and I don't mean your Hoover!).

3. Make a decision to turn some of your housecleaning duties over to the capable hands of other family members (even if they have to pry your fingers off the Dust Buster).

4. Stop making searching and fearless inventories of your cleaning supplies.

5. Admit to another human being the exact nature of your temptation to straighten stacks of magazines you pass by.

6. Make a list of all places you can strategically hide things when the doorbell rings.

> Housework, when done correctly, can kill you.
> —Anonymous

The "Dirt-free Dozen": 12 Tips for Quicker Clean-Up

1. If it ain't dirty, don't clean it. (Duh!)

2. Stubborn spots? Soak, don't scrub.

3. Keep up daily with general picking up.

4. Work from top to bottom; dust before vacuuming; and go around the room, not back and forth.

Daily? Are you kidding?

Are you an obsessive cleaner? Try not to get bogged down. Save the all-day, every-nook-and-cranny, spring cleaning stuff for...well, spring. Don't exhaust yourself; your house will still be presentable. Trust me, it will!

5 Rinse dirty dishes right away for easier clean-up.

6 Carry cleaning supplies from room to room in a bucket.

7 Tote a drawstring plastic garbage bag over your shoulder. (That's for trash, not a fashion statement.)

8 An apron with big pockets can hold bottles and brushes.

9 Delegate! Have the family draw chores from a hat.

10 Dust with a cloth in each hand.

11 Attach a long extension cord to your vacuum to save time plugging in and out.

12 Store extra bags under the one that's lining your wastebasket.

I hate housework! You make the beds, you do the dishes—and six months later you have to start all over again.

—Joan Rivers

Here's the scenario.

You just got off the phone. Unexpected guests are arriving in 15 minutes. Calm down...take a deep breath...close your eyes...now scream at the top of your lungs. There. Okay. Follow these instructions:

✓ Grab a laundry basket. Pick up the clutter. Stash the basket in a room where it won't easily be discovered.

✓ Run a feather duster over only obvious surfaces, and only if absolutely necessary.

✓ Vacuum open spaces only.

✓ Load dishwasher or just rinse dishes and put them in drainer—you can wash them later.

✓ Make sure toilets are flushed, lids are down.

✓ Wipe down bathroom mirrors, surfaces and fixtures with glass spray cleaner. Straighten towels and close the shower curtain or door.

✓ Shut all closet doors and doors to messy rooms.

✓ Light a candle or pot pourri.

✓ Oops, almost forgot. Get dressed and run a brush through your hair.

Things not to beat yourself up about:

- You haven't polished the silver since your first wedding anniversary.

- On second thought, you're not sure you've ever polished the silver.

- Come to think of it, you don't actually own any silver.

Sure, you're fastidious, but are you <u>fast</u>?

Flushed with Pride

Wherever you normally store your window cleaner (or "blue juice," as it's called in the book Speed Cleaning), stash an extra bottle and some paper towels in each bathroom. After spending a few minutes greeting your unexpected company, excuse yourself to use the restroom. While you're in there, grab the blue juice and spray, then wipe down—mirrors first, then counters and other surfaces, finishing with the commode. Dispose of paper towels and you're back with your guests, minus any worry about the state of your bathroom. There—who knew?

When you go to someone's house and it's not perfect, your first response is relief.

The ideal way to wash windows and mirrors is with newspaper and vinegar—

Yeah, if you don't mind inky fingers that smell like pickles.

And Speaking of Smells...

If you're really serious about clearing the air and baking soda just won't cut it, a commercial supplier called Neutron Industries carries industrial-strength, concentrated air freshener that will practically take care of your whole house with one spray.

"And for eliminating stubborn pet odor I recommend a product called Anti-Ickypoo, available at pet stores and animal clinics. It actually contains a bacteria that "eats up" the nasty stuff. (Funny name, great product.)"

Cleaning your house while your kids are still growing is like shoveling the walk before it stops snowing.
—Phyllis Diller

Music can move you along and help chores seem less tiresome. Keep your feather duster flying by playing Tchaikovsky's "1812 Overture" (the Lone Ranger theme song) or "Sabre Dance" by Khatchaturin (you'll recognize that one when you hear it).

"Yes, I'm expecting everyone in about half an hour. But I can't start cleaning until that last-minute adrenaline rush kicks in."

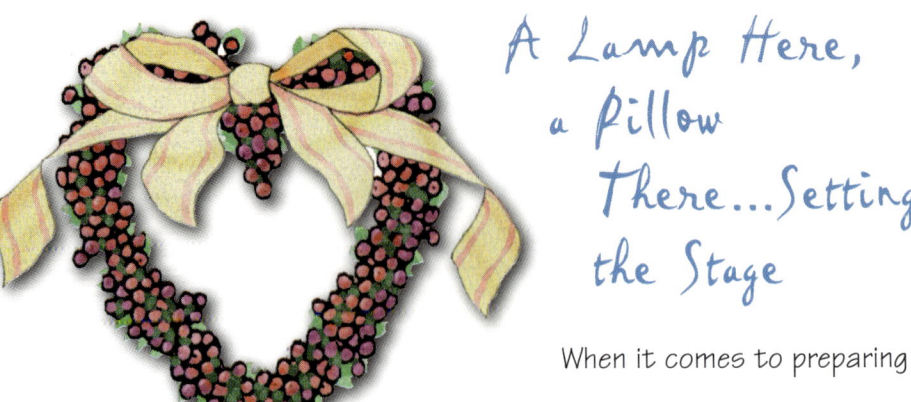

A Lamp Here, a Pillow There...Setting the Stage

When it comes to preparing to entertain, do we let home decor magazines determine our standard for having the house "company-ready"? Come on. We've all been to those homes where you're afraid to sit on the sofa because you'll mess up the pillows. And don't get me started on bathrooms with those fancy little soaps and doilies. Is anybody allowed to use those appliquéed towels? "Perfect" isn't always better. The next time you're tempted to pick up an issue of "Perfectly Beautiful So Now I Can Entertain in My Home" magazine...buy yourself some flowers instead.

> The charm of a house, like the charm of a person, is an outward manifestation of inward grace.
> —Emily Post

> *By wisdom a house is built, and through understanding it is established; through knowledge its rooms are filled with rare and beautiful treasures.*
>
> PROVERBS 24:3–4 NIV

A good exercise for preparing to entertain is to walk into your house and look around as if you were seeing it for the first time. That can be a rude awakening—especially if you've lived in the place for a while. Suddenly you realize that macramé plant hanger you made in sixth grade just may have gone out of style.... But hey, don't feel like you have to totally redecorate. The idea is not that everything has to be up-to-date and picture perfect. It's to approach your home from the perspective of "What will make my guests immediately comfortable?" Just be sure the atmosphere says, "Welcome!" and there's a pleasant, uncluttered place for them to sit.

Lord, each sense that I have is a blessing from above. May I celebrate your goodness as I fill my home with love.

—Terry Willits, *Creating a SenseSational Home*

Of course, it is possible to overdo the "first impressions count" thing.

Keep it charming, light and cheerful!

Think ahead just a little bit and set up your life to be ready for a party.

—Emilie Barnes

Innovate! Find unlikely containers for votive candles, potpourri, fruit and flower arrangements.

Instant Ambiance

✓ Burn a candle. Aroma takes people's mind off clutter.

✓ Soft music sets the tone for a relaxing get-together.

✓ Turn the lights down low to create the right atmosphere— and camouflage dusty corners!

A Little Light Conversation

Lighting can have quite an impact on your party. Did you know that people actually get quieter when the lights are lower? The owners of Radio City Music Hall found it difficult to quiet crowds in the lobby during performances until they substantially darkened the room, solving the problem immediately. So if you're going for an intimate, low-key mood, dim the lights. But for a lively, high-energy evening that gets people talking, keep it light and bright.

"Don't you think you're carrying this 'mood lighting' a little far, Amanda?"

Making Scents

If you're out of air freshener, for instant scent just sprinkle cinammon on a pan in your oven and set on low heat. Your friends will think you've been baking—ha!

Pet Peeve

As to whether Rover should be allowed to rove nearby when company comes, your friends will thank you when you care enough to send the furry beast OUTSIDE. Even little yippers can be scary—or at the very least, annoying—to non-dog people. And though most cats don't impose themselves in the same way, unfortunately, lots of people are allergic to them.

"A-a-choo!"

"Yeah, gesundheit. Whatever."

Some people are naturally cold-blooded. For them, throw a couple of afghans on the couch.

Neither Hot nor Cold

Temperature is a big part of ambiance. Don't assume that everyone else is as warm as you are—hey, you've been running around attending to things! But don't assume the opposite either.

Make Way for the Multitudes

For huge bashes, enlarge a room by moving furniture up against walls, or clearing it out if you have to. New Year's Eve in Times Square notwithstanding, the fact is that most people do not enjoy feeling crowded. If you need more seating, one option is to toss a few big pillows on the floor.

The Joneses have all their furniture out on the lawn. They must be entertaining again.

As hostess you set the emotional tone of the evening for your guests, so we strongly recommend that you take time to relax before they arrive. Take a nap or a long, hot bath—or both.

Help! I Need Some Bodies!

Worried you'll be pressed for time? Ask a friend (or friends) to help get things ready. Make the pre-party a party!

Don't be shy about borrowing the things you need. Not every household happens to own a 48-cup coffee maker and a garage full of folding chairs. Friends and neighbors are usually more than happy to come through in a pinch. Then when they need something, you get to be the hero. The sharing draws everyone closer, so it's a win-win situation.

"Are we early?"

Out on a Whim.

Be daring! Say yes to impromptu gatherings. Don't let the state of your home decide for you. After all, who really wants to give up a special evening with drop-in friends in exchange for a high-gloss polish on all the furniture?

His and Hers Approaches to Prep Work

Hers Three days before the party, she runs to the drugstore to pick out the perfect paper plate and napkin ensemble.

His Three minutes before the guests arrive, he walks to the garage to see if there's charcoal.

Hers She spends half the morning dusting the miniblinds in their home office, in case someone from the party should wander into that room.

His He spends half the afternoon playing racketball, so he can shower at the gym and get home just before the party begins.

When deciding what to wear as hostess, don't forget the all-important question of how much you want to eat and still be comfortable.

"Hmm, that little fitted number...the cotton drawstring pants...or the muumuu...?"

A celebration is...a conscious commitment to joy.

EMILIE BARNES

Chapter 3

What turns a party into a "PARTY!!!"?

Most people can easily tell when they've been to a "ho-hum" party. (It's hard to forget falling asleep with your face in the clam dip.) But what tipped the scales in that direction? Was it lack of "ambiance"? Poor lighting? Uncomfortable seating? All that stuff is important, yes. But ultimately the key ingredient is the mix of people. Their moods...compatibility...the topics they discuss. In other words, the intricate subtle human elements that make for a good party are, well—pretty much out of our control. The best we can do is plan what we think will be a good time for all, pray hard over the guest list, and hope for the best!

But wait! It doesn't have to be as scary as all that! Sure, people can be unpredictable, but there are ways to give a party the right "attitude" from the start. What you need is a wacky kind of, goofy sort of "theme" thingy, to jump-start the fun and get everybody loosened up. Read on....

"They're out of chips. Come on, let's go get our coats."

I Dunno. What Do You Want to Do?

Most of us are familiar with the basics of throwing conventional parties. But let's talk about some ideas for parties you may not have thought of before. Off-the-wall parties. Off-the-cuff parties. Off-the-beaten-path parties. Off-in-left-field parties....

> Things don't make parties. People make parties.
> —Sally Quinn

Hello, Jello™!

Here's an idea that will have you jiggling with delight! Have an all-jello menu; wear bright, sparkly, tacky jewelry and clothes that color-coordinate with your jello. Chocolate lovers can bring pudding pops. Tell your guests to go ahead and eat dinner beforehand. They don't need to worry about over-stuffing themselves. There's always room for you-know-what.

Once every couple months, have a "chick flick" night, where each person gets a turn to pick a movie. Plan your food around the movie.

God...bless us; let your face beam with joy as you look down at us.

PSALM 67:1 TLB

The Classics

For "Casablanca" we only ate black and white foods—Oreos and milk! We considered trying tea and crumpets for "My Fair Lady," but decided—authenticity, schmauthenticity!—it couldn't compete with double fudge chocolate brownies.

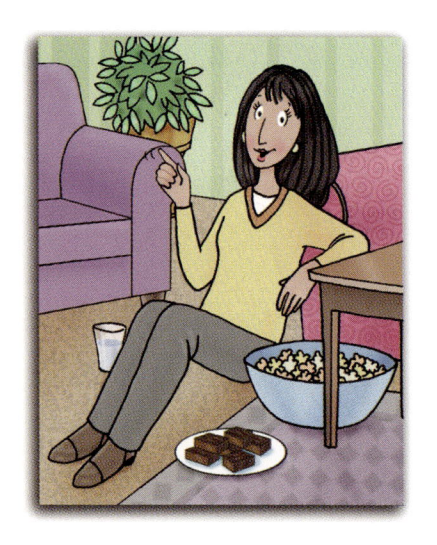

To Dye For

A "true colors" party is a real Girls Only proposition. It's a marathon of nail painting, clothes—and hair?—dyeing...you can even have your make-up and wardrobe colors analyzed. Great idea for a sleepover!

Now That's Weird...

When Mia finally recovered from her foot surgery, she decided to celebrate by throwing a Foot Party. She served foot-long hotdogs (sole food) and toe-fu (an alternative to finger sandwiches). We played a game to see who could pick up and carry the most items with their toes! Mia supplied pedicure kits and polish, then held a "Most Beautiful Feet" contest.

"Looking for Louvre"

Have everyone meet at an art gallery and form a museum scavenger hunt! It requires a little upfront planning, but could be lots of fun. Afterwards, wind up with lunch at an "artsy" café.

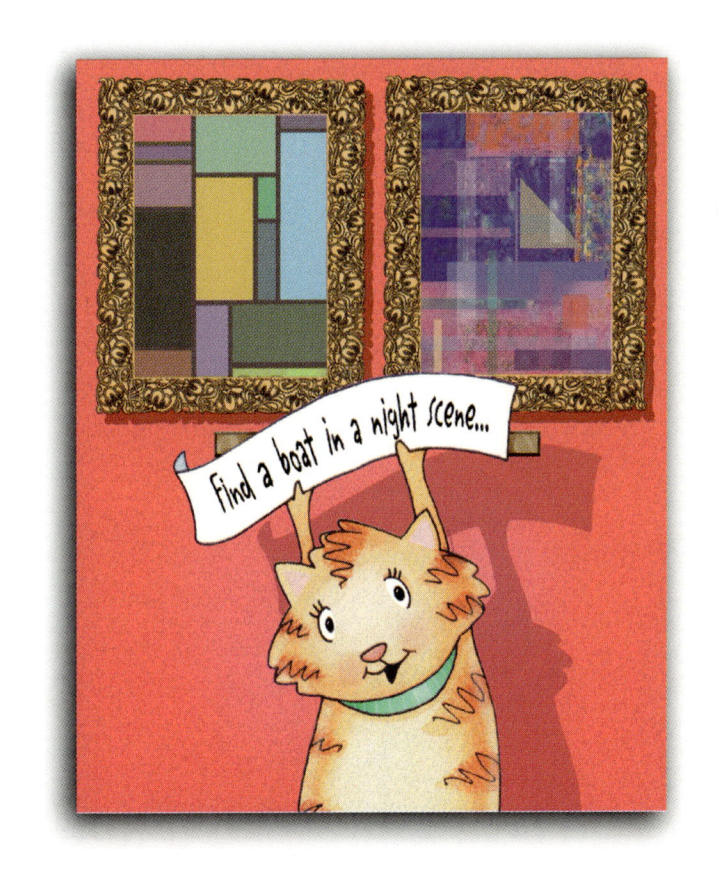

Find a boat in a night scene...

Beyond Fun and Games

A party can also be an occasion to remember the needy. Get together to share an act of kindness.

- Do yard work or housework for a shut-in.
- Collect canned goods for a local food shelf as a "ticket" to your party.
- Volunteer your time as a group for a worthy cause.

A Simple Party "Favor"

With parchment paper and a calligraphy pen, write out Scriptures or special blessings for each of your guests (for example: "I love the way you..." or "Thank you for all the times you..."). Roll them into little scrolls tied with ribbons or raffia.

Theme parties to avoid:

✓ The Indoor Mid-Winter Beach Party—who wants to be seen in a bathing suit in the dead of winter after gorging on holiday food for four months straight?

✓ The Dysfunctional Family Reunion

✓ The Wrestlemania Costume Party Marathon

✓ The Bring-Your-Favorite-Rodent Party

I like this one!

When Food Is the Guest of Honor

Begin an annual tradition! Some families get together to make apple butter in the fall, build gingerbread houses for Christmas, or have a clambake in the summer. What a great way for generations to mix, mingle and make memories—and friends are as welcome as family.

For Brave Souls Only!

Here's a risky idea for the hostess with a sly sense of humor. Send out fancy invitations...lead your guests in every way to believe they are attending a very stiff and formal dinner party. But when they arrive, instead of utensils they will find only large cloth napkins...with plastic gloves rolled up inside! Once they've figured out this is all they've been given to eat with, you serve the main course: spaghetti! (The cloth napkins will come in handy here!) You'll see a lot of people who were prepared to mind their manners loosen up and really enjoy themselves! P.S. Better have the number of a good dry cleaner on hand, just in case.

"A bag of ice would have been fine, Wanda. You didn't have to go all out!"

"Specialized" potlucks you may not have thought of...

- ✓ A monochromatic (all one color) menu—a fun change of pace and an artistic challenge for everyone!

- ✓ Ask your guests to bring the dish they're most proud of—along with copies of the recipe for others to take home.

- ✓ Oodles of Noodles—a feast of pasta dishes, hot and cold...pasta salad, linguini, lasagna... (Plan to make it an early evening—the entire gang may be sound asleep by 8 o'clock!)

One way to make a party effortless is to get your guests to do a lot of the work for you! Hence, the popularity of potlucks.

Ready or Not?

My husband brought home unexpected company for a dinner party. ONCE.

"Will I Have to Drive in Reverse?"

You've heard of a progressive dinner, right? That's where each course is served at a different person's home. Tired of the expected? Try the alternative—a regressive dinner. Wear your clothes backwards and have dessert at the first house, salad at the last.

A Moving Event

Give a "house cooling" party if you're saying goodbye to a well-loved home. Save yourself the trouble of a moving sale by offering each guest a "white elephant" gift as they depart. (It helps if all your friends drive mini vans!)

When I moved to Minneapolis, my friends threw me a Mary Tyler Moore party! Everyone dressed in Mary-chic or Rhoda-funky, and the living room TV ran back-to-back videos of the show. We topped off the evening with a farewell "hat toss!"

How Many Candles Can You Handle?

I have one thing to say about "Over the Hill" parties with black balloons and jokes about how ancient we're getting. Stop it! I'm getting too old and cranky for this! I say we celebrate our age! In fact, when I turn 40 I'm going to throw my own party.

Ideas for a "We're Not Getting Older, We're Getting Better" party:

- ✓ Sing karaoke to the music you loved best as a teen (or play the 45s if you still have them!).

- ✓ To prove that we're never too old to have role models, salute some famous person you admire who is older than you...and who you want to be like "when you grow up!"

- ✓ Pass around baby pictures of each other and play a who's-who guessing game.

Surprise! Surprise! Surprise!

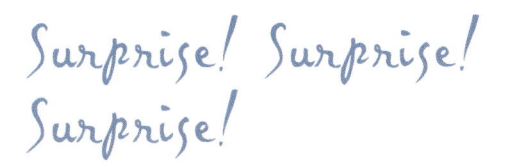

Try a progressive approach to a surprise party, by moving from surprise to surprise. The guest of honor is swept along in a state of constant anticipation as each gift or event shows her how much you care.

1. A singing "Happy Birthday" telegram shows up at her door (not the kind you find in the yellow pages—enlist a friend who can carry a tune!).

2. A chauffeur-driven limo (or sedan) whisks her away to a restaurant or movie theater, where more friends are waiting.

3. You stop off at the local store to "pick up a few things"; you've arranged for her to be paged to the service desk where a bouquet of flowers awaits her!

4. Cake and ice cream are served in the park, while a violinist (another musical friend perhaps?) serenades her with her favorite tunes.

A big advantage to this approach is that if you blow one surprise, you still have others in store!

"God help me through the holidays, let nothing me dismay! Remind me, Lord, that all this stress pays off on Christmas Day!"

Ho-Ho-Honing Your Seasonal Skills

There are scores of books out there on how to do up the holidays right. All we have to say on the subject is this: If you have never experienced an "effortless" yuletide, give yourself a tremendous gift this Christmas. Toss your cares like tinsel on a blue spruce…give up the hurry and worry…lighten up and just for this one year, do things the easy way. Grab that plate of home-baked cookies your neighbor blessed you with, and go party at someone else's house!

At Christmastime, brighten up your table by placing ornaments at each place setting with guests' names painted on them.

Until I was eight years old, I thought everyone had lutefisk for Christmas. A Scandinavian dish made from raw fish soaked in lye, lutefisk has been described as "the piece of cod that surpasses all understanding." You either love it or you loath it. Either way, it makes for an interesting (albeit, slimy) conversation piece.

All Things New

Coming up with New Year's resolutions can be a challenge, but a really enjoyable one—when you're doing it for someone else! Draw names and swap resolutions with your friends for the coming year. ("I will try to limit my desserts to three a week—unless it's cheesecake." "I will read at least six good pieces of literature this year—and one without pictures!")

From the Heart

Valentine's Day doesn't just have to be romantic. It's also a time to show your friends how much you care about them. This is your chance to throw the best party of the year— the "Don't Come through My Door Unless You're Carrying Chocolate" party.

Mocha mackerel?

Shower the People You Love with Love

If you've been to many wedding showers, you've probably noticed one thing about the guest of honor: she's stressed. Happy... glowing...yes. But definitely stressed. One of the nicest things we can do for our bride-to-be friend is not to buy her another silver serving tray—it's to help simplify her life. Assemble a memory album—with pictures and personal notes written by all her friends. This is something she can keep and cherish for years to come...and it never needs polishing.

The key to a great wedding or baby shower is to make sure the guest of honor doesn't have to do a thing but show up. Consult with her close friends and family while planning the details, not with her.

Incredibly Silly Baby Shower Ideas
(But aren't they all?)

- ✓ Throw Scattergories dice (the kind with letters) or choose Scrabble tiles to create imaginative baby names for the mother-to-be.

- ✓ Bobbing for Pacifiers!

- ✓ Pin the Diaper on the. . .

"Don't even try it!"

Rejoice with those who rejoice.

—ROMANS 12:15 NIV

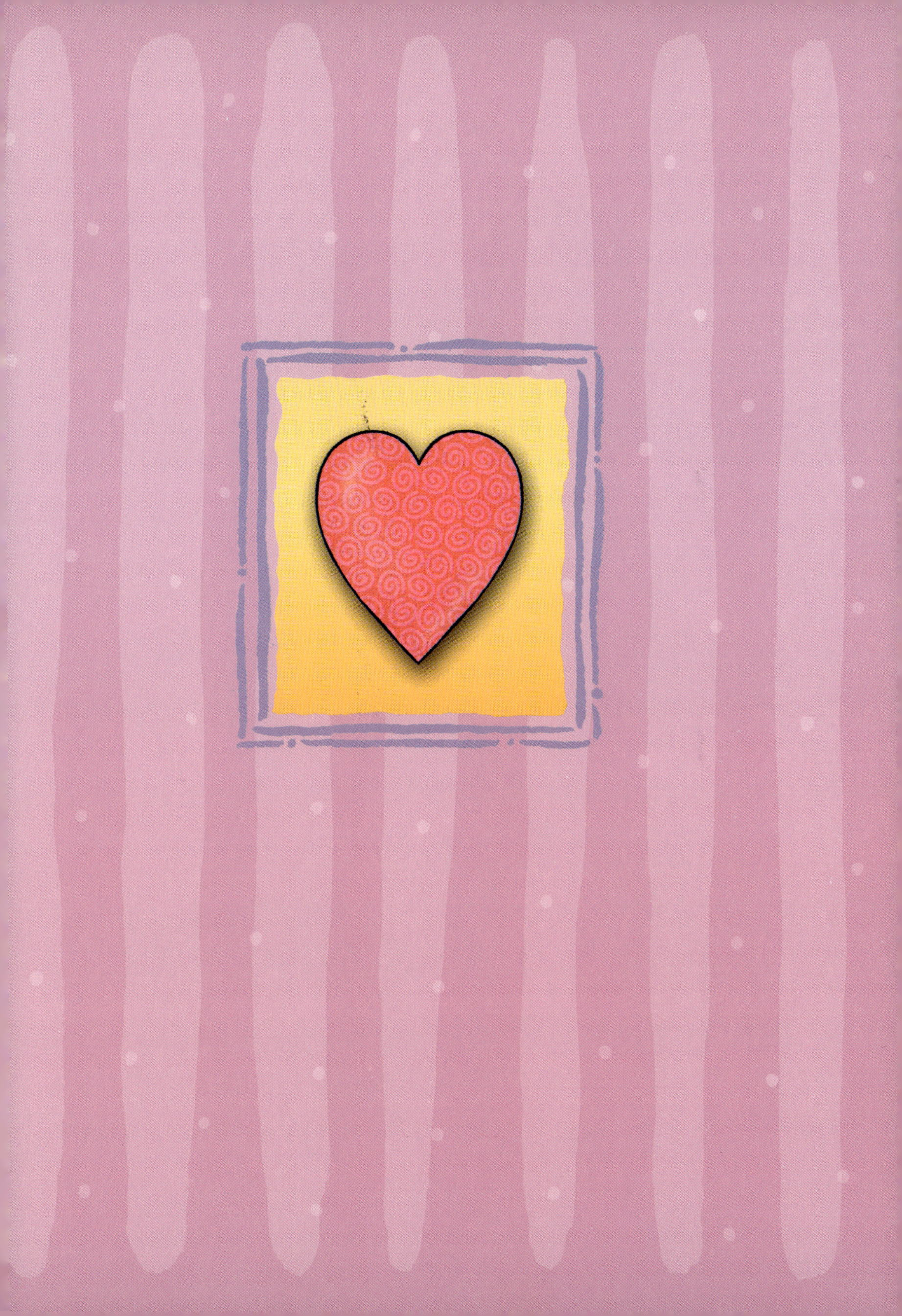

"We could get pizza!"

Chapter 4

Eat, Drink and Be Merry—for Tomorrow Somebody's Gotta Clean Up this Mess

It's My Party and I'll Fry If I Want To

So far we've convinced you that entertaining doesn't have to be scary, that you don't have to spend a month getting ready, and that some party ideas are just too much fun not to try. So what's the hold-up? Why haven't you run to the phone and started gathering a crowd for the weekend? Oh, yeah. The "C" word. C-O-O-K-I-N-G. Well, relax, girlfriend. First of all, there are other options. The yellow pages are filled with wonderful restaurants. Then there are caterers. (And that doesn't have to be expensive; sometimes a friend who loves to cook can make the best caterer of all.) And don't forget, you can always go potluck. A sign-up sheet is a must if you don't want to end up with all desserts. (On second thought, that may not be all bad.)

Where Are You in the Potluck Hierarchy?

Gourmet-made-from-scratch-handed-down-through-the-generations-family-recipe dish

Whipped-up-the-night-before-from-stuff-you-had-on-hand casserole

Chips and a two-liter picked up at convenience store on the way to the party

If you have a husband, convince him right from the start that outdoor grilling is the domain of the hunter-gatherer male. He feels rugged and manly; you get out of cooking. It's a win-win thing.

Cooking from scratch is an admirable thing. But where in the world do you buy "Scratch"?

Wherever you go, whatever you do—always make friends with the cook.

—John Ratzenberger

Did You Know?
By the time she is 45 years old, the average woman has spent over 50,000 hours in the kitchen. And we wonder why we can't lose weight.

I have a Six Month Rule for kitchen gadgets. If it sits for half a year without being useful, baby, it's history!

10 Stupid Things Women Do to Mess up Their Kitchens:

1. Keep only one set of something that's used all the time (salt & pepper shakers, for example).

2. Fill their cupboards with extra salt & pepper shakers and other useless space hoggers.

3. Clutter counter space with seldom-used appliances.

4. Banish seldom-used appliances to the back of a cupboard to gather cobwebs.

5. Locate spices too near the stove. (Heat is not conducive to their longevity; spices stay fresher in a cool, dry place).

6. Store spices in a cool, dry place but neglect to use most of them because they aren't out in the open near the stove.

7. Meticulously choose the freshest, loveliest fruits and vegetables in the produce department, then stash them in a crisper drawer and end up forgetting they bought them.

8. Display fruit and vegetables in artistic, colorful arrangements on their table...until the one on the bottom ends up bruised and mealy and they all have to be thrown out.

9. Stash melon ballers, fondue pots and fragile china in unreachably high cupboards or in the dark recesses of drawers.

10. Throw away the melon baller, fondue pot and fragile china the week before they decide to give a formal fondue party with a melon ball dessert.

Serve one another in love.

GALATIANS 5:13 TLB

Kindness and consideration go much further in making your guests feel comfortable than do all the perfectly flambéed peaches in the world.
—Emily Post

A successful party is one where everyone has a good time—including the cook.

"I just love cajun cooking.
What a great excuse to burn everything."

Aahh, the challenge of creating something out of nothing!

The fewer ingredients we have available, the more ingenuity we're forced to exercise and the prouder we feel if the results happen to be spectacular!

"Beyond Measure"

Consider learning the skill of cooking "to taste." It's like playing music by ear—a totally liberating experience!

Be original! Explore! Experiment!

Live dangerously!

I know how to live on almost nothing or with everything. I have learned the secret of contentment in every situation.

PHILEMON 4:12 TLB

"I have a recipe. It involves puncturing the plastic to allow the steam to vent."

Chapter 5

Now We're Cookin'...

Hors D'oeuvres, Canapés, Appetizers, Crudités...Just Hand Me Something I Can Eat with My Fingers

Hors d'oeuvres are something of a lost art. People worry about the fat content and spoiling their appetite for dinner. But there's a quality in tiny, personalized, bite-size items that makes us feel really special. If they're cute and original, we exclaim over them like little girls over a dollhouse.

"Simple rule of thumb: Don't cook what you can't pronounce."

I need a quick recipe... and I need a recipe—QUICK!

If you want to go to the trouble of dusting off the cookie cutters, try these clever little sandwiches: Cut partially frozen sliced bread into decorative shapes. Make a small cut-out into the shape on top so you can peek through to the sandwich filling.

We may live without poetry, music and art;

We may live without conscience and live without heart;

We may live without books;

But civilized man cannot live without cooks.

—The Earl of Lytton

Thou shall not double dip!

> Love is sweet, but it's nice to have bread with it.
>
> —Yiddish Wisdom

Ready-Made Dip

1 carton ready-made dip
1 crystal or antique bowl
1 green onion, chopped (optional)

Open dip, dump into bowl. Using a fork, fluff the dip. Top with a sprinkling of green onion or other garnish (this makes them wonder if you made it yourself). Serve with veggies or chips.

Dill roll-ups

1 pkg. thinly sliced corned beef (or other deli meat)
Cream cheese
Baby dill pickles
Toothpicks

Spread a thin layer of cream cheese on corned beef. Line 1 or 2 pickles (use the straightest ones) on one edge of the meat and roll. Cut into ½ inch sections. Spear with toothpicks and serve on a lettuce lined platter! You may want to use more than one slice of meat per roll.

Recipes

Shrimp Wedges

6 puffy pita bread
2 Tbsp. olive oil
1 Tbsp. grated parmesan cheese
1 tsp. garlic powder
1 1/2 c. grated mozzarella cheese
1 pkg. frozen salad shrimp (thawed)
1 can artichoke hearts (chopped)

Mix olive oil, parmesan cheese, and garlic together. Brush or drizzle about 1 tsp. on each pita bread. Arrange shrimp and artichoke hearts on bread. Top each with 1/4 c. mozzarella cheese. Bake at 400 degrees for 7 to 10 minutes, just until cheese is melted and bubbly. Cut into wedges and serve warm.

Cheesy Bruschetta

1 loaf sliced French bread
1 clove garlic, cut in half (or garlic powder)
1 c. chopped plum tomatoes
1/2 c. each mozzarella and provolone cheese
1/4 c. chopped green onions
2 Tbsp. parsley

Arrange bread slices on large cookie sheet and toast in 400 degree oven until browned. Remove and rub each slice of bread with cut side of garlic (or sprinkle with a little garlic powder). Mix the rest of the ingredients in bowl. Spoon onto bread slices. Bake at 400 degrees for 8 to 10 minutes, just until cheese melts. Serve hot.

Fantastic French Bread

1 loaf French bread
8 slices of Swiss cheese
1/4 c. softened butter
1 tsp. onion powder
2 tsp. poppy seed

Cut French bread into slices diagonally, but not completely through the bottom. Combine onion powder, poppy seed and butter. Spread into slices. Place 1/2 slice cheese between slices of bread. Wrap in foil and bake in a 350 degree oven for 10 minutes. Serve piping hot!

Thirst Quenchers

Keep some sort of fruit juice on hand for guests. It can be punched up by adding 7-Up or club soda—or think healthy and drink it straight up!

Even if you are not a coffee or tea drinker, keep them on hand for company, especially overnight guests who rely on their morning "eye opener."

Pink Lemonade

Lemonade, preferably with pulp
1 small jar maraschino cherries
Ice

Fill large pitcher about half way with ice. Add lemonade and full jar of cherries with liquid. Mix briskly. Serve in tall glasses. Garnish with lemon slices and cherries.

Which Is Hotter?

Just when you've invested $180 for a top-of-the-line cappuccino maker and developed a taste for latté—guess what? Coffee's out. Tea's in. Yep. Never since that famous tea party in Boston has tea been so popular this side of Liverpool.

> He who refreshes others will himself be refreshed.
> —PROVERBS 11:25 NIV

Of the several ways to make a good cup of coffee, sheer accident is as good as any.

"Marie, dear, use your imagination. You'll need to serve more than just cakes!"

Chocolate Cracker Crunch

chocolate chips or almond bark

Ritz crackers

peanut butter

These are so-o good and so-o easy. Simply spread peanut butter on a cracker and top with another cracker. Dip this "sandwich" into melted chocolate chips or almond bark (follow package directions). Lay on wax paper to cool. Enjoy!

No-Bake Cookies

2 c. sugar

1/2 c. butter

1/2 c. milk

1 tsp. vanilla

3 c. oatmeal

6 Tbsp. cocoa (unsweetened)

1/4 tsp. salt

Bring to boil: sugar, butter, milk, vanilla, and salt. Boil 2 minutes, stirring from time to time and lowering heat to avoid burning. Remove from heat. In a large bowl, combine oatmeal, cocoa, and salt. Stir in mixture from pan. Drop by spoonfuls onto waxed paper and allow to cool. (Optional: 2/3 c. coconut or 1/4 c. peanut butter.)

Recipes

Can You Boil Water? Then You Can Make Caramel!

Caramelizing. Sounds practically exotic, doesn't it? Something you would only find in some fancy magazine by someone with the initials...oh, I don't know...M.S. maybe? Ha! This process is deceptively simple. It's just sugar that you almost burn—but not quite. Adding butter transforms it into a rich, golden sauce. Try it—on ice cream, popcorn, apples, pound cake, pretty much anything...

Take ordinary granulated or powdered sugar, mix with just enough water to liquefy, and dissolve completely. Then heat to boiling, but once it boils do not stir, just swirl the pan around. When it achieves a translucent golden color, take it off the stove and set the pan on ice.

Cheesecake Hearts

2 c. crushed graham crackers

1/4 c. sugar

3 Tbsp. butter or margarine, melted

3 (8-oz.) pkg. cream cheese, softened

1 (14-oz.) can sweetened condensed milk

3 eggs

2 tsp. vanilla

Preheat oven to 300 degrees. Line 13x9 baking pan with heavy foil. Combine crumbs, sugar, and butter. Press firmly into bottom of pan. Mix cream cheese in bowl until fluffy. Gradually add in milk. Add eggs and vanilla; mix well. Pour over crust. Bake 45 to 50 minutes or until set in the middle. Chill at least 1 hour or overnight. Use foil to carefully lift cake out of pan. Cut into heart shapes with cookie cutter or knife. Serve with caramel or chocolate sauce drizzled on top.

Grasshopper Pie

(This pie is so rich it makes Bill Gates jealous.)

1 pkg. crushed Oreos

1 (12-oz.) can chocolate syrup

1 gal. mint chocolate chip ice cream (The green kind makes it really grasshopper-y!)

Crush Oreos for the bottom layer. Add chocolate syrup, then mildly thawed ice cream, followed with some more crumbled cookies. Top with more chocolate syrup. Refreeze for one hour. Believe me, it's worth the wait.

No Fail Easy Fudge

18 oz. semi-sweet chocolate chips
1 can sweetened condensed milk
1 ½ tsp. vanilla
Dash of salt

In a square microwave-safe pan, heat ingredients together until all are melted, mixing occasionally. Add chopped nuts (optional). Refrigerate until firm enough to cut into squares.

Ice cream: enemy of the hips, friend to the lips...and the lips get first dibs, so they usually win!

Death by Chocolate

Brownies (make from a mix, from scratch, or purchase already made)

2 small boxes instant chocolate pudding (make according to directions on box)

1 large container of whipped cream

4-6 candy bars (crunchy ones are better, Hershey bars, Butterfingers, etc.)

½ c. pecans

Tear brownies into bite-size pieces. Put half of the brownies in the bottom of a large glass bowl. Top with half of the pudding, then half of the whipped cream. Crumble half of the candy bars and nuts on top. Repeat layers. Chill. Serve cold.

"Fondue Is Fun to Due"

Easy fondue ideas:

- ✓ dip marshmallows into melted chocolate chips

- ✓ dip mandarin orange slices into almond bark (low guilt factor here—there's fruit inside the chocolate)

- ✓ dip apple slices into caramel sauce (see the previous caramel sauce recipe— make with butter)

- ✓ dip other fruits (bananas, strawberries, nectarines) into any sauce!

Wherever your treasure is, there your heart and thoughts will also be.

—LUKE 12:34 TLB

Summer Angel

Angel food cake (already made)

1 small box instant vanilla pudding (made according to directions on box)

1 small container whipped cream

1 tsp. orange zest

4 c. fruit, sliced as necessary (berries, kiwi, peaches, etc.)

Gently mix pudding with orange zest and one cup whipped cream. Slice cake into 1/2 inch slices. Lay one slice on plate. Top with pudding mixture. Arrange fruit on pudding. Top with another slice of cake. Garnish with more whipped cream and a piece of fruit, if desired. (This recipe can be served to friends that are dieting. Just use low-fat or no-fat whipped cream, sugar-free pudding, and skim milk. Tastes great on the lips, looks good on the hips!)

> One of the secrets of a happy life is continuous small treats.
>
> —Iris Murdoch

Delicious DESSERTS
(That's S-T-R-E-S-S-E-D Spelled Backwards)

Things to keep in the pantry or the freezer in case guests suddenly appear at dinner time:

- ✓ Brownie mix
- ✓ Snack crackers
- ✓ Chocolate chips
- ✓ Candy bars
- ✓ Cans of sweetened condensed milk
- ✓ Ice cream
- ✓ Peanut butter
- ✓ Boxes of instant pudding
- ✓ Graham crackers
- ✓ Frozen whipped cream

(If you don't feel up to making dessert, just arrange some of these things on a platter and enjoy!)

> We dare not trust our wit for making our house pleasant to our friend, so we buy ice cream.
> —Ralph Waldo Emerson

Good manners sometimes means simply putting up with other people's bad manners.

H. JACKSON BROWN

Chapter 6

If I Take My Elbows off the Table My Head Will Fall Down: Practical Etiquette for the New Millennium

— from The Ladies Home Journal, 1883

As a rule, it is well to be slow about calling upon strangers, say one's new neighbors, for it is sometimes difficult to become rid of undesirable acquaintances, and a lady does not wish to slight anyone. Calls should be made within three days after a dinner, or an entertainment of any kind if it is a first invitation, and within a week after a party or ball...

Living in a Post-Emily Post World

I don't know about you, but I just don't give a whole lot of thought to the finer points of proper etiquette. Filling my head with a lot of do's and don'ts just makes me nervous. I worry that I'm going to embarrass myself, and when I'm nervous—I usually do!

"So which side of the Post fence are you on?"

I'm thankful that we live in a more casual day.... But on the other hand, I sometimes wish for that more refined time, when ladies were ladies and gentlemen held the door open. We don't want to toss all the rules out the window, do we?

What times! what manners!
(O temporai! O mores!)

CICERO

"Let's see here, Joan is allergic to lobster hair and can't eat cats—or is it the other way around?"

I always keep a record of what I served to whom for future reference, so I won't be embarrassed by preparing the same dish twice.

Good way to safeguard yourself against food poisoning law suits too. "No, Your Honor, at that particular meal I did not, in fact, serve half-cooked chicken. It was the week before."

Hmm. Yes, well, that does bring up a good point. Check with guests in advance to see if there's anything they can't eat.

A little simplification is the first step toward rational living.

"When I was 18 I tried to help out my aunt Betsy by washing her cut-glass serving dish (dismissing her polite plea, 'Oh, no, don't wash that. I'll do it.') Of course I dropped it and it shattered. There was dead silence as she held up the broken pieces. Then, never saying a word about its age or value, to make me feel better she told me, 'I never liked that old thing anyway.' Later I found out it was a 120-year-old family heirloom. Now, is that class or what?"

Yeah, "bad manners" is all relative, right? And if you met my relatives you'd know what I mean.

True graciousness extends itself beyond the rules to make you feel at home.

Many women do noble things, but you surpass them all.
—Proverbs 31:29 NIV

Many points of etiquette vary from culture to culture. For instance, the Japanese consider it basic politeness to partake of everything that is offered. We don't expect that in America. If you turn down her homemade cheesecake, your hostess is less likely to feel offended than to admire your self-discipline!

Did You Know?

> Schools of etiquette produce it by training; love does it by instinct.
>
> —Henry Durbanville

Did You Know?

Contrary to popular belief, "RSVP" does not stand for "Reply Soon with Victorian Punctiliousness" (or "Rarely Shoot Victims of Procrastination"). But it's French for essentially the same thing: Répondez, s'il vous plaît (please respond).

Paper or ~~Plastic~~ China? Formal or Non?

For a formal party you need...

- ✓ strategic guest mix
- ✓ attractive table, properly set
- ✓ gourmet menu
- ✓ flawlessly-prepared food
- ✓ competent servers
- ✓ printed invitations, three weeks in advance

For an informal get-together you'll need...

- ✓ a working phone
- ✓ a few spontaneous friends
- ✓ comfortable space to spread out and enjoy one another's company

> Guests would do well to remember that the unwritten rule about being fashionably late still applies.

"Oh, great! Wouldn't you know they'd be on time!"

Reality-based entertaining means we're comfortable letting our guests see the way we really live.

When the party is large enough to need servers, hire your friend's teenage daughters or local college students. But allow a little time for training on some basic serving etiquette.

"I'd Like You to Meet What's-His-Name..."

Ever stumped for the right way to introduce people? I used to get so flustered from wanting to do it properly. You know, do I introduce from left to right, or tallest to shortest? One time this really got the best of me. I was at a company function and I began to introduce my husband to a co-worker and forgot his name! My husband's, not the co-worker's! I smiled sheepishly, looked at my husband then introduced him as "the man in my life." My husband still ribs me about that one!

Good help is so hard to find.

How Do You Do the How-Do-You-Do's?

There are not a lot of rules anymore about how to make proper introductions. Just remember to use both people's names in each introduction: "Sue, this is Alice. Alice, this is Sue." This gives them two chances to hear each other's names. The only hard part of this is making sure you know both names. If you have to ask? No big deal—even if it's your husband.

No matter how formal the event, the fine old tradition of piling coats on the bed is something we can be thankful for—some of us more than others!

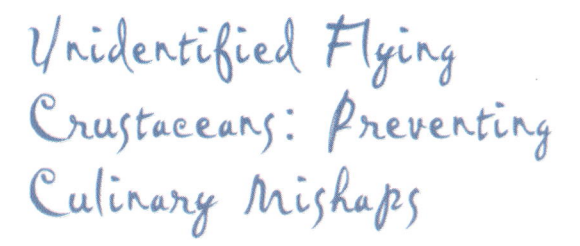

Unidentified Flying Crustaceans: Preventing Culinary Mishaps

Ever since she cracked open a crab leg in a restaurant and the meat flew across the room beaning an unsuspecting patron on the forehead, Julie has become acutely aware of potentially hazardous food choices. In menu planning, keep in mind that easy-to-eat dishes set guests at ease, and lap food in particular should not require much cutting or fancy fork work.

Washington hostess Sally Quinn suggests that if you're nervous or intimidated playing hostess, you should picture your guests naked. We wouldn't suggest it at the table, however. Not if you want to keep your appetite.

"Let's see... when I stand I serve from the left, remove from the right. So when I'm sitting, do I pass to the left if I'm sitting on the right?"

As a guest the uppermost thought is, roughly: I'd better behave so they will ask me again. As hostess: she had better behave if she wants to come back. Yes, I think I'd rather be hostess.
　　　—Ruth Stout

If you're passing serving dishes around the table, they go counterclockwise—from your left to your right. It's that simple. But if you get the mashed potatoes and gravy going in two different directions, what's the worst that can happen? A tasty collision?

Did You Know?

The butter plate is smaller than the salad plate and is placed above the forks while the salad plate, if served with the entree and not as a separate course, is placed to the left of the forks.

Now we will have tea. Sit down carefully and don't grab.

young Daisy
(alias Mrs. Smith)
of *Little Men*

P.S. Did you care?

I'm sorry, Gwenyth. You and Charles will have to leave. You've upset the delicate balance of our dinner party by using your dessert fork for the shrimp cocktail.

Confused about which utensil to use at a formal dinner? Work your way toward the center with each course. If you have a particularly stimulating dinner partner, you may lose track of your silverware altogether. Would that be so bad?

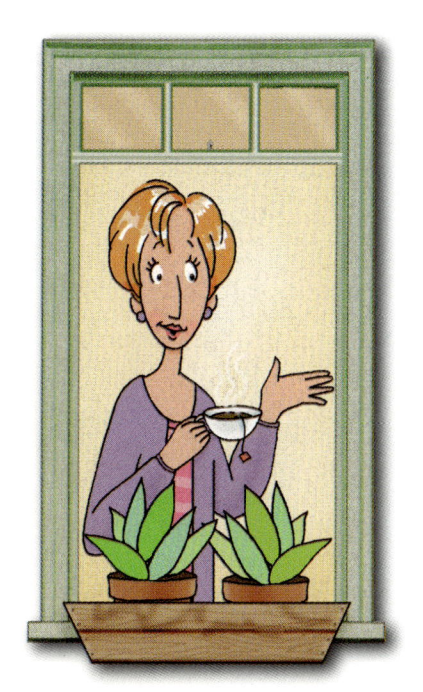

After I've been invited to someone's home or out to eat, is it necessary for me to "reciprocate in kind"?

Reciprocate in any way you want to. Even Emily Post allows that an evening of fine dining can be repaid with bowling and pizza if the mood strikes.

Exasperated, the Swansons finally resorted to charades as a clever ploy for getting rid of guests who couldn't take a hint: "Two words...first word—Go!... second word—'There's no place like _____'...'Lady Bird, Lady Bird, fly away _____'...'Sounds like comb!'...

Gracious Good-byes

Here are a few polite phrases for subtly letting guests know it's time to hit the road:

- ✓ (With a sigh) "I wish we'd had more time to visit..."

- ✓ From the classic movie "The Women," "I'm afraid I'm keeping you."

- ✓ In the spirit of true Southern hospitality, "Y'all have a safe trip home now, y'hear?"

- ✓ And from Pride and Prejudice, in Jane Austen's inimitable style, "You've delighted us long enough."

> Manners are a sensitive awareness of the feelings of others. If you have that awareness, you have good manners, no matter what fork you use.
> —Emily Post

May the Lord keep watch between you and me when we are away from each other.
—GENESIS 31:49 NIV

When you've been here an hour, you're not compay anymore.

EDWINA SUTTON

Chapter 7

As Long as You're under My Roof... Helping House Guests Feel at Home

To Each His Own

What's the right way to behave with house guests? Do we stop everything to be at their beck and call, or go about our everyday activities and leave them some free time? Perhaps there's no one approach that's best for everyone. The Golden Rule ("Do unto others as you would have them do unto you") doesn't exactly apply, because what's comfortable for one person puts another ill at ease. To find out how your guests prefer to be treated, I guess you just have to ask!

> Honest communication is the key to taking the guess-work out of guest-work.

"Could you fill these out in triplicate? We want to optimize your comfort level during your stay."

An overnight "guest basket" can include:

- ✓ a night light
- ✓ pot pourri
- ✓ fresh towels and a bath mat
- ✓ little travel-size bottles of shampoo, lotion, etc.
- ✓ bubble bath
- ✓ candles
- ✓ fresh flowers
- ✓ magazines

> Every house where love abides and friendship is a guest is surely home, and home sweet home; for there the heart can rest.
>
> —Henry Van Dyke

Out-of-towners appreciate your input on places to go, since you know the area. If you want to show them the town but not monopolize their vacation, give them a list of choices for sight-seeing, museums, etc., and suggest they rank them in order of preference. It's okay to make recommendations, but leave it up to them how they spend their time.

For I was hungry and you gave me something to eat, I was thirsty and you gave me something to drink, I was a stranger and you invited me in.

Matthew 25:35 NIV

One of the biggest nightmares with house guests can be figuring out what to feed them. Should you go the "knock 'em dead" route and serve seven-course meals with fresh flowers and a violinist? Or the "grab-whatever-you-can-find...my-fridge-is-yours" route? Well, how about a little of both? Stock the house with foods that can be used either as snacks or as meals—like cold meats, cheeses, breads, and fresh fruits. These can be put out and people can serve themselves buffet style at their leisure. For the fancier fare, why not try a favorite restaurant in town? Delivered pizza by candlelight is always fun too!

> We welcome you most cordially.
> We welcome you most regally.
> Frank Baum, "The Wizard of Oz"

Ring Bell
for
Service

"From 12:37 to 1:13 we will peruse the antique book store. After that we will take a brisk walk downtown, followed by three minutes free time!"

> "Stay" is a charming word in a friend's vocabulary.
>
> AMOS BRONSON ALCOTT

You can get pamphlets on local attractions from your city's visitors' center. Put a stack of them in the guest room, just like a bed and breakfast. (Be careful though...too many "local attractions" and they may never leave!)

The most thoughtful thing you can do for your house guests is simply to let them know how happy you are to be with them.

"Mi casa is su casa. Mi husband is su son!"

Victoria, suddenly overcome by a case of nerves, becomes silly in front of her in-laws.

Having your in-laws stay should be no big deal. They're just like anybody else...except that they'll be watching every little move you make and remembering it for life.... Just kidding!

Even the nicest in-laws are only slightly less scary than outlaws.

Leave family albums in guest rooms. Having them displayed or within easy access to guests may be preferable to forcing your friends—out of politeness—to sit through a guided tour of photos in which they recognize few people. Some love it, others don't. (Could be a perfect way to get rid of guests who've overstayed their welcome!)

"Oh, wait! Wait! Don't go to sleep yet! We're only through the slides up to grade school!"

She gleans how long you wish to stay; She lets you go without delay.
—The Ideal Hostess

She is not difficult to please;
She can be silent as the trees.
She shuns all ostentatious show;
She knows exactly when to go.
—The Ideal Guest

Cheerfully share your home with those who need a meal or a place to stay for the night.

1 PETER 4:9 TLB

Do not forget to entertain strangers, for by so doing some people have entertained angels without knowing it.

HEBREWS 13:2 NIV